Drama Workshop Plays
Edited by Dan Garrett

Friends and Neighbours

Listen to the Pin Drop
Dan Garrett

I Could Wring Her Neck
Julia James

I Tell a Lie
Michael Maynard

Hands Off!
Marianne Cook

Published by arrangement
with BBC School Radio

M
MACMILLAN

First published 1984
Reprinted 1985 1986, 1991

Published by
MACMILLAN EDUCATION LTD
Houndmills, Basingstoke, Hampshire RG21 2XS
and London
Companies and representatives
throughout the world

Printed in Hong Kong

British Library Cataloguing in Publication Data
Garrett, Dan
Friends and neighbours.—(Drama workshop plays)
1. Children's plays, English 2. English
drama—20th century
I. Title   II. Series   822'.914'08   PR1272
ISBN 0–333–36054–0

Preface

Drama Workshop Plays are intended for 11 to 13 year-olds
to read or to act in class or in groups. They have been
adapted from scripts originally written for the BBC radio
series *Drama Workshop*. As broadcast, the scripts were
deliberately incomplete, to act as springboards for classroom drama. In these versions, new scenes have been
written, and the plays are complete in themselves.

Each volume contains four plays grouped under a broad
thematic heading. The plays have been chosen for their
variety in content and style, and for their suitability in
different kinds of classroom or drama club use. Some are
realistic and down-to-earth, others are historically based,
or are ventures into some kind of (often ugly) future. The
first play in each volume is usually closest to the everyday
drama of young people's own lives; the plays that follow
become progressively more demanding.

Some of the plays have large enough casts for most
young people in a class to have a different part. Others are
more suited to group work, but a whole class can easily be
involved if different groups work on different scenes. The
play can then be read or performed with each group doing
its scene in succession.

For English work, teachers will find *Drama Workshop
Plays* suitable for reading and for discussion, and to spark
off playwriting. For drama, teachers will find them a useful
introduction to scripted work since they allow plenty of
scope for improvisation, and they have a free-flowing form
close to the idiom of young people's own drama. The more
ambitious may wish to rehearse the plays and perform
them in a workshop setting, or record them as radio or
video plays. Most of the plays make a point about some
social or moral issue which can stimulate a variety of
follow-up work. For this reason teachers will also find them
valuable for RE. Full notes on using the plays are at the
back of each volume.

Contents

About the writers

Dan Garrett started work in the theatre, has had wide drama teaching and lecturing experience, and is currently a Senior Drama Producer with BBC School Radio.

Julia James was seventeen when she wrote this script. She was commissioned by BBC School Radio after her earlier play, *Me I'd like to Kill Miss Kerr*, reached the finals of the Royal Court young playwrights' competition.

Michael Maynard is an actor with many theatre and television credits, and a writer who has devised pieces for several Theatre-in-Education teams, especially Greenwich Young People's Theatre, and Theatre Centre. He has written for *Drama Workshop* for the past seven years.

Marianne Cook taught drama for a number of years. She is now a freelance writer with many School Radio scripts and published plays to her credit.

Introduction

Life would be a lot easier if we could all be good friends
and good neighbours. There would be far fewer quarrels
for a start. Somehow, though, it is easier said than done,
perhaps because we're so sure we ourselves are always the
very best of friends or the very best of neighbours to those
around us.

In *Listen to the Pin Drop*, the three families each
consider themselves ideal neighbours. Somehow the others
don't share that view, especially of the Rowdie family —
but it's hard on rowdy families who find themselves living
next to people who are as 'quiet as church mice'.

Friends can be so good to us — when we don't want
them to be — that we can end up feeling we could wring
their necks. Other friends become pains in the neck because
of an unfortunate habit — like telling lies.

Good neighbourliness is not simply a matter for
individuals. We all live under the shadow of giant businesses
and industries, and we rely on them to be good neighbours
and not pollute us, nor make our lives unbearable in other
ways. In *Hands Off!* a village tries to protest against its
planned extinction, when it is destined to be flooded as
part of a reservoir scheme. There is no great secrecy, and
people will be offered compensation, and other people
far away will benefit greatly, but it's not the sort of
neighbourliness we'd like thrust on us.

Listen to the Pin Drop

by Dan Garrett

Cast: **Jim Rowdie**
Doreen Rowdie
Nicola, their daughter
Eileen Pindrop
Harry Pindrop
Sonny Uppendown
Liz (Miz) Uppendown

1 *The action moves between three flats in the same block, and the balcony between them. The Pindrops.*

Eileen: The house I live in must be calm and peaceful. It must be so quiet you can hear a pin drop.

Harry: *(Whispering)* Yes, dear.

Eileen: I said, calm and peaceful!

Harry: Yes, dear, I heard you. And I answered.

Eileen: You mumble, that's your trouble.

Harry: *(Mumbling)* Yes, dear.

2 *The Rowdies. Loud music: rock or heavy metal.*

Nicola: *(Shouting)* That's what I like!

Jim: *(To no one in particular)* DIY? Don't talk to me about DIY! Every weekend there's something else to be seen to. This place is falling to pieces. *(Kicks a chair)*

Doreen: *(Rescuing it)* Jim! You don't have to help it!

(The music cuts)

3 *The Uppendowns*

Sonny: Look on the bright side, Liz Miz, that's my motto!
Liz: Don't you call me miserable: I'm not. I just got out the wrong side of the bed this morning and everything since has been at sixes and sevens. How I shall cope with it all, Sonny, I do not know . . .

Sonny: Take a tip from me: every cloud has a silver lining!

(Liz turns away in exasperation)

4 *The Rowdies. We hear the loud music again. Doreen is washing up with a good deal of clatter.*

Doreen: Nicola! Nicola! *(Nothing happens)* Nicola! Turn it down! *(Still nothing happens)* Oh – that girl! Jim! Where are you?

Jim: Here I am.

(He enters and noisily sets down a big tool-box)

Doreen: Jim!

Jim: What is it, Doreen?

Doreen: Can't you hear?

Jim: Oh, her. *(Bellows)* Nicola!

(The music abruptly comes to an end. Pause.)

Jim: Now we can hear ourselves think. What I had in mind,
Doreen, was to fix the new sink.

Doreen: What, now?

(The music starts again — a new track)

Jim: That's the limit. Nicola!

(The music stops again)

Jim: Yeah, the sink. So move over . . . No, leave the washing
up.

Doreen: But I'm in the middle — Jim, how can you be so
inconsiderate?

Jim: Right, here goes . . .

(He starts an electric drill with hammer attachment)

Doreen: I've got too much to do. You'll have to stop.

(A pause. He doesn't stop. Doreen slams out.)

Nicola: *(Hardly audible above the drill)* Dad. Dad!

Jim: *(As he turns off the drill)* Who's that?

Nicola: *(Still shouting from off stage)* Dad, how dare you!
How can I hear myself think? I've got my exams.

Jim: What do you mean, got exams? I've got to do this. Been
hanging over my head for months . . .

Nicola: *(Protesting)* Oh, Dad . . .!

Doreen: *(Re-entering)* What's up now?

Jim: *(Still to Nicola)* And what about your music? How you can work with all that row going on . . .?

Nicola: It's not row, it's a very modern sound.

Doreen: You're supposed to be revising.

Nicola: So? It helps me concentrate.

Doreen: Do what?

Jim: Don't give me that.

Nicola: It's true.

Jim: *(As he starts up the drill again)* Never.

Nicola: Dad! Oh . . .

(She's back in her room, slamming the door. The drill continues, joined by her music.)

5 *The Pindrops. Harry is dozing under a newspaper. The drill and music can still be heard, but slightly muffled.*

Eileen: Dear. *(He doesn't respond)* Dear! *(He lifts the newspaper)* Dear, you really must go and say something. We can't let it go on. Can we? *(He's dozing again)* Lift that newspaper and listen.

Harry: I don't want to listen.

Eileen: But they'll blast the walls down. And they'll have your picture of Loch Lomond off the hook — the one you took so long putting up. And what about the little porcelain figurine that Aunt May gave me as a wedding present? The vibration rattled it right off the shelf. *(Harry is dozing again)* It was worth a lot of money. Mrs Thompson told me. *(A sound — a snore? — from under the newspaper)* What, dear?

Harry: *(Asleep)* Yes, dear.

Eileen: Thoughtless people. You must tell them. Mustn't you, dear? Dear, mustn't you?

Harry: *(Reluctantly lifting the newspaper)* With regret, dear, I don't see how I can go round this time. I mean, before, there was a definite cause for complaint. We had the evidence, so to speak.

Eileen: The figurine all in pieces. I wept.

Harry: I know you won't agree with me, but I think we should bear up a little longer. Remain patient. Until the time is ripe.

Eileen: Time is ripe, indeed!

Harry: *(Firmly)* Yes, dear.

Eileen: Nonsense.

Harry: *(Meekly)* Yes, dear.

Eileen: I can't think what I saw in you. I always said you should have been more like my brother Lawrence. He'd go round. He'd tell them.

(The music stops)

Eileen: What, dear?

Harry: I didn't say a word.

Eileen: No. And I sometimes wish you would. Particularly at a time like this. I'd like to believe that just once in a while you could stand up for us. Behave like a real man. Instead of sitting there in your slippers.

Harry: Yes, dear.

Eileen: You'll go to your grave saying, 'Yes, dear'!

(Next door, an extremely loud track begins)

Eileen: That's it. I've had enough. My nerves won't stand a moment more. You've got to go, Harold. Out the door.

Harry: But . . .

Eileen: Not a word. Go and tell them.

Harry: But, my dear, are you sure it wouldn't be better if you went? After all . . .

Eileen: Harold, don't say a word more! Who is the man in this house?

(He smiles at the thought that really she is. Eileen doesn't notice.)

Eileen: Very well, then. Go on.

(That wipes the smile off his face)

Harry: Yes, dear.

(He goes out reluctantly, and turns towards the Rowdies' flat. He hesitates, plucks up courage to knock, thinks better of it, and goes back down the corridor to the Uppendowns', ducking as he goes past his own flat so that Eileen can't see him. He knocks and Sonny answers.)

Sonny: Harry, old chap. How nice to see you. Things going well, are they? You're looking a picture of health. Come on in.

(They go in and Sonny closes the door. We, of course, can still see and hear them.)

Harry: *(To Liz)* Good morning.

Liz: What's good about it?

Sonny: *(Brightly)* Now what can we do for you, old chap?

Harry: It's the noise. Electric drills, washing-machine, that awful music . . .

Liz: Oh, that's ever so bad. That's really terrible. I don't know how you can put up with it.

Harry: My wife can't.

Liz: All that noise must drive your poor wife out of her mind. And it'll get worse, you see.

Sonny: No, no, look on the bright side, that's my motto. Things have got to get worse, and then they get better. You see.

Harry: But my wife's health is suffering. I've got to tell them, she says. And I don't think they'll listen to an old man like me. So I thought that maybe . . . If you're troubled by the same noise as well . . .

Sonny: Can't say I am, exactly, no.

Harry: Ah, but if there were the two of us . . . . It'd make more impact. I mean, both of us at their door, telling them . . . .

Sonny: But it's not my quarrel, old chap. Keep your nose out of other people's business and all that.

Harry: I wouldn't think of it as interfering.

Sonny: No, but they might.

Harry: Oh dear, I don't like making a fuss. I'll say the wrong things and that'll make them unpleasant. Threatening, maybe. And I can't bear threats or unpleasantness. I easily get upset. So couldn't you . . . If you'd only come with me . . .

Sonny: You're worrying far too much. Be firm with them. Explain what it's like living with their noise. Now off you go . . . *(He's half-pushing Harry to the door)* Strike while the iron's hot . . .

(As he opens the door, we hear drill, music, washing-machine)

Harry: Yes, well thank you. Goodbye.

Sonny: So long, old man.

(Sonny closes the door. Harry goes reluctantly to the Rowdies' front door and stands there dithering.)

Sonny: What a coward.

Liz: He won't stop them. His wife'll be putting up with that noise for a good bit longer yet.

Sonny: He's caught between the Devil and the deep blue sea!

6 *Outside the Rowdies. The drill and music are very loud.*

Harry: I wonder if I dare knock? I'm sure they'll be as fierce as they sound. Oh, what shall I say? I think I'll go back home. But then I'll never hear the last of it from Eileen. She'll go on, nag, nag, nag. My life won't be worth living – I'll have to knock. *(He knocks timidly)* Oh dear. Once more. *(He knocks louder. A pause.)* They haven't come. Right then, this is it. *(He knocks very loudly, and jumps back startled at himself. Pause.)* They still haven't come. And after I'd keyed myself up to it. What will I tell Eileen?

(He lets himself into his own flat. The drill and music are still very audible.)

Eileen: What have you come back for?

Harry: Just for a moment, dear.

Eileen: But you haven't stopped it.

Harry: No dear. I did knock . . . *(She stares coldly at him)* Three times. But they didn't answer. I knocked very loudly, dear.

Eileen: Harry. I do not know how you dare come back and look me in the face. Words fail me. Harry. Do you hear? Now, do I have to get up, put my things on and go and fetch my brother Lawrence to do your dirty work for you, or are you going to go back there and tell those people what you should have told them ten minutes ago?

(Pause)

Harry: I'm going to go back, dear.

Eileen: That's more like it. And when you get back we can have a nice cup of tea together, can't we?

(Harry smiles weakly and goes. Drill and music up. Again, after nearly going to the Rowdies' flat, he ends up at the Uppendowns'. Sonny lets him in.)

Harry: I'm at my wits' end. They didn't hear me knock, and now Eileen has been very cross with me. Please can you help?

Sonny: What can we do, old chap? Your best bet is to look on the bright side. Every cloud has a silver lining.

Harry: That's all very well, but how long will it go on for?

Liz: Yes, Sonny, that's all very well, but I couldn't live next to that row. These walls are paper thin. No, once a thing like this starts, you never know where it's going to end.

Sonny: That's your pessimism speaking.

Liz: For once I know I'm right. It's all very well, you chirruping around, but our two poor neighbours have to put up with a situation that's getting quite out of hand.

(We begin to hear rock music, and the drill)

Sonny: I shouldn't worry. A month or two, and I'm sure things will start to improve.

Harry: What's that?

Liz: Oh no! It can't be. Not through two lots of walls.

Sonny: Probably temporary. A window open.

Liz: That's the limit. I agree with Harry. We've got to put a stop to this once and for all. *(To Harry)* I'll back you up.

Sonny: No need to get worked up, Liz Miz. It won't last for ever.

Liz: Take no notice of him. Come along, Harry.

(As they open the door and cross to the Rowdies' door, the noise becomes unbearable. Harry hesitates, but Liz bangs loudly. Nothing happens.)

Liz: I wonder if it was right to come. I don't expect they'll even hear us.

Harry: Perhaps we should give up. I really don't know what to say. And I'm sure they'll be unpleasant. Shout at us, even. Let's leave it.

Liz: I knew they'd never come. It's a hopeless task.

(Suddenly the drill stops)

Liz: Oh. One last go, eh? I'm not very optimistic, but we've got to try.

Harry: As you say, we have to try.

(Liz bangs again)

Liz: Do you know, I'm beginning to sound like my husband. Got to try, indeed. That's just what he'd say.

(Jim opens the door and there is a further increase in the music)

Harry: Ooooh!

Liz: Come back, Harry!

Jim: What do you want? *(Shouting)* What? What is it? Hey, Nicola! Turn that row down, will you? Nicola!

(The music stops)

Jim: That's better. Now. Yes?

Harry: Well, you see . . .

Liz: It's the noise. Things have gone from bad to worse. First it was the Pindrops – I mean Harry and Eileen – they . . .

(A washing-machine starts to spin clothes)

Jim: Doreen! You can't spin the washing now, I'm talking. Doreen! *(To Liz and Harry)* Wait a minute. *(He calls back)* There's someone at the front door. Now leave it.

Doreen: And when do you expect me to get all the washing on the line, eh?

Jim: Not just at this moment.

Doreen: Oh, Jim!

Jim: No!

Doreen: You're always stopping me from doing things . . .

(Jim and Doreen continue to argue while Liz speaks to Harry)

Liz: Have you ever heard anything like it?

Harry: I think I'd rather listen to the drilling.

Jim: Sorry about that. Spot of bother. It's over now.

Liz: *(To Harry)* Go on. You have it worst. You say.

Harry: I can't . . .

Liz: You can. You've got to.

Jim: Yes?

Harry: You see . . . Oh dear . . .!

Liz: Go on.

Harry: It's like this. My wife and I live next door. We're very quiet people. Secluded. We like a bit of peace now and again. Don't get me wrong — we don't expect everyone to be as quiet as church mice. But we do feel we're entitled — especially now I've retired — to just . . . just a modicum of peace and quiet. Newspaper over the head, feet up for an afternoon nap and that kind of thing. If you follow me. Once in a while . . .

Jim: *(To Liz)* You're not his wife. Who are you?

Liz: No, I'm not his wife. I live one door further down. And the noise, your noise, is penetrating. We hear it, even.

Jim: The walls are paper thin.

Liz: I say exactly the same. And that's why we deserve a little more consideration.

Jim: I see. *(He calls back inside)* Doreen! *(To Harry and Liz)* I think something can be done.

Doreen: What is it?

Jim: We've got the neighbours round complaining.

Doreen: I'm not surprised.

Jim: Exactly. Nor am I.

Doreen: We're terribly sorry.

Jim: Indeed we are.

(Liz and Harry exchange triumphant looks)

Doreen: You call her, Jim.

Jim: Right, I will. Nicola! Nicola, come out here at once!

(The music is turned off. Silence. For the first time.)

Jim: Do you hear?

Nicola: All right, Dad. What is it? *(She sees Liz and Harry)* Oh!

Jim: The neighbours, that's what. Complaining about your noise.

Liz: *The* noise!

Jim: *(Not following her)* What?

Harry: It's my wife. She's getting ill with it. You'll have to stop.

Nicola: Dad, Mum . . .

Doreen: Don't take it too hard, dear. You must admit, it was very loud. Even Dad has had to speak to you about it.

Harry: We're not telling you not to play . . .

Doreen: No dear, you can play it softly.

Jim: Got that Nicola? *(Shouts)* Softly!

Nicola: Yes, Dad. *(She goes back inside)*

Jim: Sorry about all that. She's a good girl, really. But they're all the same over music at that age. The louder the better.

(The music has begun again. Loudish.)

Jim: Nicola!

(The music is turned down. Still audible.)

Jim: There. She'll give no more trouble now. Settled then, is it? Good. I must get on.

Liz: But it's not only the . . .

Jim: Morning.

(He shuts the front door. Nearly a slam.)

Harry: Oh.

Liz: I don't think it is settled . . .

(The washing-machine and electric drill start up again)

Harry: Oh, no.

Liz: Here we go again.

(She knocks loudly, and Nicola opens the door)

Nicola: Oh, hello. What is it?

Liz: Listen. That's what it is.

Nicola: *(Beginning to chuckle as she realises her dad is in for it)* I see what you mean. Dad's not going to like this. Dad!

Harry: Oh dear. Really, I ought to be getting along . . .

Liz: You're not going now. We're half-way there.

Nicola: *(Bellowing)* Dad!

(The drill stops, then the washing-machine)

Liz: And we're not stopping now.

Harry: I suppose you're right.

Liz: I know I am.

Jim: Who is it, Nicola? Oh — what is it this time?

Liz: It's the noise. It's as bad as ever — very nearly.

Jim: What? *(To Nicola)* What you giggling for, Nicola? Have you turned that record up again?

Liz/Harry: No, she hasn't. It's not her.

Jim: Then just what is it you're after?

Harry: It's the — the other noise.

Nicola: He means your drill, Dad.

Jim: What? But that's only an ordinary drill.

Liz: Ah, but the walls are paper thin.

Jim: What?

Liz: You said so yourself.

Jim: This is not on. I'm trying to do the flat up, and it can't be done without some noise.

Harry: We don't want total quiet.

Jim: Then what do you want?

Harry: Couldn't we come to some agreement?

Jim: An agreement?

Liz: That's right.

Harry: Perhaps if it was either Nicola's music — quietly, you understand — or the drill, but not both together.

Jim: *(Scratching his head)* Phaw . . . difficult.

Liz: Even Sonny and I can hear you. Two doors down . . .

Jim: Suppose I've no choice. Right, it's a deal. You hear that, Nicola? That's you an' all. Get it? Every time I drill, you turn the music off, right?

Nicola: Oh, Dad! That's ridiculous! Why can't you use your drill when I'm not playing music. . . .

Jim: And how will your mum get her new sink?

(Nicola is momentarily stuck for an answer)

Liz: Well. Now that's sorted out, we won't take any more of your time.

Jim: Oh – er, you off, then? Right.

Harry: *(As he and Liz leave)* Thank you. Thank you very much indeed.

Jim: Now look, Nicola, that's all your fault . . .

(He shuts the front door, and we can only see, but not hear, the remainder of the quarrel)

Harry: *(At the door of his flat)* And thank you, too.

Liz: Don't mention it! But we'd better keep our fingers crossed.

(They both go into their own flats)

7 *The Pindrops*

Eileen: You got them to turn it down, then? It took long enough. I thought my nerves were going to burst. I said to myself, I'll give him five more minutes, and then I'm off to the doctor. I'd have had to have some more of those pills again. Sedatives. And you know how they knock me out. You'd have had to do the housework. I couldn't have.

Harry: *(With new-found confidence)* Make me a cup of tea, dear, to celebrate.

Eileen: What?

Harry: Make me a cup of tea.

Eileen: But I was only telling you . . .

Harry: I know. But now I've stopped the noise, I want some peace. I'd like to hear a pin drop. Wouldn't you?

Eileen: *(Getting up for the first time)* Oh! Oh yes, dear.

Harry: Good. And one more thing. Liz Miz, I mean Mrs Uppendown, helped me out. And it didn't seem right — my neighbour's wife, not you. Another time, you will back me up, won't you?

Eileen: Oh — yes. Yes, dear!

Harry: *(Triumphantly)* Good.

8 *The Uppendowns*

Sonny: It's all turned out for the best, then.

Liz: Ah, but it might not have done. I had to feel so miserable that I *had* to get up and do something.

Sonny: There you are, like I always said . . .

Together: Every cloud has a silver lining!

(Blackout/curtain)

I Could Wring Her Neck

by Julia James

Cast: **Janice**
                 Reda
                 Mike
                 Allen
                 Dave
                 Mr Redford
                 Various members of the class, and friends of Janice

1 *In the front of Jan's house — either a hallway or a front room. Then on the way to school.*

Jan: *(Off stage)* Just coming, Reda, I shan't be long. I'm just brushing my teeth, okay?

Reda: Honestly, Jan, it's twenty past eight already. Even if we leave now we're gonna be late.

Jan: *(Still off)* So what, Reda? If we are gonna be late, we might as well do it in style, okay?

Reda: Okay, okay, I'm sorry, just remember your words next time *you* call for *me*. *(Pause)* Are you listening to me, Jan?

Jan: *(Entering)* Of course I am, Reda, when have you known me do otherwise?

Reda: Do you really want me to tell you?

Jan: Okay. Point taken, and what are you doing just standing there? Like you said, if we don't leave now we are going to be more than late. *(Jan opens the door for Reda and calls back)* 'Bye, Mum!

(She slams the door behind her and starts to go off. Reda deliberately hangs back.)

Jan: Come on, Reda. You are the one who said we were going to be late — so just stop standing around and move, okay?

Reda: *(Still hanging back, but walking to school now)* What a cheek! Honestly, Jan, you've got a nerve. *(There's something she's leading up to)*

Jan: Me! You are saying that *I* have a nerve?

Reda: I don't care how sarky you get, 'cos I've got the edge on you today. Honestly, Jan, you really are rich. I mean to say, Jan, at least I always turn up *even* if I *am* late. After all, better late than never — like you last night. You never turned up.

Jan: *(Calm)* Well, actually I had thought up a really *sound* alibi, but then I thought I had better tell my best friend, Reda, the truth, the whole truth and nothing but the truth.

Reda: *(Sweetly)* So?

Jan: Reda, you know that I tried to ring you last night to tell you that I could not come, but you had already left.

Reda: You rang at 7.30. You knew that I would be outside the pictures waiting for you.

Jan: Yes, I knew you would have left by that time, but you see I wasn't allowed out last night.

Reda: What a load of trash, rubbish, garbage! You could have thought of something a little more original than that. I *know* why you didn't come last night.

Jan: Oh yes, why?

Reda: I know, Jan, that you went to the youth club last night instead of going to the pictures with me. But what I really want to know is —

Jan: *(Interrupting)* Oh, Reda, you're joking!

Reda: Jan, Jan, Jan, you haven't even got the shame to feel ashamed, or even a little embarrassment.

Jan: Reda, just how did you find that out? Nobody was supposed to tell you. I'll kill whoever did it!

Reda: Well, your mum is still at home, and I am *sure* your kitchen knives are sharp enough to do the trick. Okay?

Jan: *(She is not pleased)* Sometimes my mum just doesn't know when to keep that mouth of hers shut!

Reda: Jan, what d'yer go to the youth club for, eh? I mean it must be something good to get you that brilliant shade of embarrassment.

Jan: Brilliant is an underestimation! But as for why I went in the first place, if you do not know already, I ain't gonna add to my embarrassment by telling you.

Reda: I somehow didn't think you would, so I'll see you in class, okay? *(Makes as if to go off, but Jan stops her)*

Jan: *(In a tone of voice which says, 'You're not going to like this, but I'll tell you anyway')* Reda, wait . . . You're not going to like what is going to happen in class, but you *are* going to enjoy the result. So remember what you always say . . .

Reda: *(Interrupting)* What *you* always say: 'The means *always* justifies the ends.'

Jan: *(Appeasing)* Yes!

Reda: See ya in class, Jan. And remember how vindictive I can get!

(Exit Reda, enjoying herself, followed less enthusiastically by Jan)

2 *Jan and Reda in their classroom. The bell goes for registration. Their teacher has not arrived yet, but the rest of the class are present. Jan has just entered and puts the register on the teacher's desk. She walks over to Reda.*

Jan: How about this for timing, Reda. Perfect, wouldn't you say?

Reda: We only just made it, madam.

Jan: Ooh, I really have got your back up over the cinema last night — have I not? *(Laughing)*

Reda: *(Interrupting her)* Now, now, just a minute, Jan, stop for a moment and explain what you're up to. I ain't got what you're talking about.

Jan: *(Laughing through her words)* Have no fear. All will be revealed!

Reda: Jan, lady of mystery, please reveal all quickly, as I think that I have become the lady of little patience. Get it?

Jan: All I hope is that you appreciate what I am doing for you – all the trouble I went through on your behalf. But, why am I saying this? I know what an appreciative little friend you are. *(She bursts out in sarcastic laughter at this point and then composes herself)* Now Reda, all you have to do is sit back and find out what I was up to last night, okay?

Reda: Jan, why don't I like the sound of this?

Jan: Reda, this is very embarrassing. Everyone knows that you fancy someone like mad. It is so obvious it's sickening. So as I am your best friend I decided to do something about it.

Reda: *Jan! Jannn!* Did you ask Dave if he fancies me?

Jan: No.

Reda: *(Not believing her)* Oh God, you didn't tell him that I fancy him, did you?

Jan: No.

Reda: *(Still suspicious)* Well?

Jan: Well what?

Reda: Well what did you do then?

Jan: Well . . .

Reda: *(Interrupting her)* Did you say anything to him?

Jan: No.

Reda: You mean you haven't done anything?

Jan: No.

Reda: *(Guessing that something horrible is about to happen)* Gawd, Jan, I know what you've done.

Jan: Well, a bit of patience will tell you all.

Reda: How would you like to die, my dear? *(Accusingly)* You told Allen, didn't you?

Jan: No.

Reda: No?

Jan: No.

Reda: No?

Jan: No, definitely no.

Reda: Who did you tell then?

Jan: Mike *and* Allen.

Reda: Oh!

Jan: You see, I was so fed up with you mooning over Dave, so I decided to do something about it and I needed their help, okay?

Reda: Okay. *(Pause)* Okay? Their help — how?

Jan: Simple. *(Shouting)* Mike, Allen, over here.

Mike: Seems like the moment of justice for them has arrived.

Allen: *(Fake American accent)* Sure thing, pardners.

Mike: Shut up, Allen. You have nothing constructive to say.

Allen: Okay, pard.

Mike: You see, Reda, it wasn't only Jan who was fed up with a mooning friend, so were we. The point is, if you and Dave get together then you will be doing us a favour. You two can moon over each other at the same time, in private, by yourselves.

Allen: Hey shucks pard, you're embarrassing the little lady, Mike.

Jan: Shut up, Allen, just remember the plan, okay?

Allen: Sure thing, Jan.

Reda: Hey, stop a mo'; Jan, this is me you're talking about. Your best friend? Why don't you tell me what this plan is before you start on it, eh? Now ain't that a good idea?

Jan: Reda, dear if you had spoken sooner we might have considered it, but as it is, the plan is already in motion and we have not got the time to explain it to you. Now, all we want you to do is answer the next few questions as truthfully as possible, okay?

Reda: Yes. But . . .

Allen: *(Interrupting)* First question.

> *(They start to play a game — well rehearsed at the youth club — in which Allen is the master of ceremonies, Mike a kind of prosecutor and Jan keeps order. The class participates in the game, laughing, whistling and egging it on.)*

Mike: Name?

Reda: Reda.

Allen: Second question.

Mike: Age?

Reda: I'm . . .

Jan: *(Interrupting)* Reda is a lady so you *never* ask her her age.

Allen: Third question.

Mike: Sex?

Reda: Female.

Allen: Fourth question.

Mike: Nationality?

Jan: Have you got one?

Reda: Yes.

Allen: Time for contestant number two.

Jan: I think the next one is called Dave.

Reda: Jan, you are going to regret this! *(She sounds as if she is fighting a losing battle to contain her anger/revenge/ hysterics. As she speaks Dave is 'escorted' to the seat next to her. But he does not sit down.)*

Jan: *(Laughing)* No comments from the contestants, please!

Reda: *(Through her teeth)* Jan . . .

Allen: Here we have him, folks. All the way from the boys' loos down the corridor, con-tes-tant numero duo. It's our very own, well loved *(Aside)* by Reda. *(Loud)* Wait fooorrr i − t . . . *(Shouted)* Dave! *(Cheers and clapping from the rest of the class)*

Jan: Dave, here, have this seat next to Reda. *(Whistling and giggling from the class)* Questions, please.

Dave: Hey, wait a mo', what's going on?

Jan: You see, Dave, it's all very simple.

Dave: It is?

Mike: YES!

Jan: You see, the point is that Mike and Allen, your best friends, decided to do something for your own good. They got a little bit fed up with your mooning over a certain person not a million miles away from you. So we, that is, Mike, Allen and myself, Jan, decided that it was time something positive was done to encourage a romantic situation between yourself and the lady in question. So just answer the following questions as quickly as possible.

(Allen and Mike speed their questions up)

Allen: Question numero uno.

Mike: Name?

Dave: Dave.

Allen: Question numero duo.

Mike: Age?

Dave: You . . .

Jan: *(Interrupting)* Next question.

Allen: Question numero trezo.

Mike: Sex?

Dave: Male.

Allen: Question numero quatro.

Mike: Nationality?

Dave: Yes.

Jan: Well done. Now that didn't hurt much, did it?

All Three: Stage Two.

Mike: This stage was my idea, so I am going to be master of proceedings. Is my cast ready?

Allen: Sure thing.

Jan: Yes.

Mike: And my audience, you're all ready and . . .

The rest of the class: WAITING!

Mike: Dave?

Dave: *(Reluctant)* Yes.

Mike: Reda?

Reda: *(Resigned)* Yes.

Mike: Now Dave, Reda. I will be asking the questions and all you have to do is repeat the answers after Allen and Jan respectively. Okay?

Dave:
      Together.
Reda:

Mike: Now for the first question. Who is/are your best friend/ friends?

Allen: Mike and Allen are my best friends.

Dave: Mike and Allen were *(Allen thumps him)* sorry, *are* my best friends.

Jan: Jan is my best friend.

Reda: Jan is *(?)* my best friend. *(Jan, not pleased by Reda's tone of voice, looks very cross)*

Mike: Will the contestants please note that they are supposed to repeat everything in their answer exactly. Okay?

Dave: *(Resigned)* Okay.

Reda: *(False obedience)* Okay.

Mike: *(Over-sweet)* Good. Right, the next question. How long have you had these particular best friends?

Allen: I have been best friends with Allen and Mike since playschool, where we all met.

Dave: I have been best friends with Allen and Mike since playschool, where we all met.

Jan: I have been friends with Jan since we were babies, as our mothers were both in hospital at the same time and they became friends and then we did.

(The class do a sweet 'Oh!' — as in 'Oh, isn't that nice!')

Reda: I have been friends with Jan since we were babies, as our mothers were both in hospital at the same time and they became friends and then we did. *(The class repeat their sweet, 'Oh!', but Reda cuts them off)* Unfortunately.

Mike: Now now, Reda, that was not very nice, was it?

Reda: No.

Mike: Good, now for a crucial question — who is the most attractive person in this room? Remember, you don't have to be objective, just give us your opinion.

Allen: Reda.

Dave: Reda.

Jan: Dave.

Reda: Dave.

Mike: GOOD. Now . . .

Jan: For . . .

Allen: Part . . .

Jan: Stage . . .

Mike: Section . . .

Allen: Three. Shucks, folks, Stage Three is where a subtle, gentle, considerate, kind young man is needed, and that's why I got the job.

Mike: Just get on with it, Allen, okay?

Allen: Okay. Just because you're jealous. Anyway, the moment has come for Dave to ask Reda the question we have all been waiting for. Come on, Dave. . . . We are waiting, Dave. . . . Do your duty, okay?

Dave: Allen, Mike, Jan – my friends? Have you never heard of privacy?

Allen: Hey pal, we're waiting, okay? So do your duty.

Dave: Reda, I was going to ask you some time in the future in PRIVATE, but my arm has been twisted, so . . . Would you like to go out with me?

Jan: Now, Reda, don't answer straight away. Keep him waiting for a while, while you make up your mind, okay?

Reda: I think – I know – I would have preferred PRIVACY, but as Jan would put it, beggars can't be choosers, and the answer is yes, now what's the question? *(Lots of cheers and clapping from the rest of the class)*

Jan: You will not regret this, Reda. Of that I am positive.

Reda: So am I. I won't regret it, BUT you will, just mark my words. I'm out for revenge, my *best* friend.

Jan: So you are to be avoided for the next few days.

Reda: Yes, you are going to regret this — making a public spectacle of me!

Jan: Reda, I know you were a little embarrassed, but I did it for your own good — and you were always being embarrassed by the rest of the class when you were mooning over Dave.

Reda: So what? I have a plan brewing for you.

(The bell for lessons goes. Exit Reda.)

3 *Same classroom. Afternoon registration.*

Jan: And who were you with at lunch, Reda?

Reda: You and the rest of the school know exactly where I was at lunchtime; we never got a moment's privacy.

Jan: Reda, you spoke to me!

Reda: I know. But we all make mistakes.

Jan: Come off it, you just can't resist my charm! And besides you like talking to me. Also, as Dave gets the register in the afternoons, you can't very well go off with him.

Reda: *(Overdoing the sweetness)* Look, Jan, what I said earlier about never wanting to talk to you again, well, that was just the heat of the moment and I didn't mean it, honestly.

Jan: I knew you did not mean it but . . .

Reda: But?

Jan: But Reda, you are being much too nice to me. I mean this morning while you were thinking of some . . . thing to do to me you weren't talking to me and now you are. Reda —

this is Jan, your best friend. *(Nervous laughter)* What are you going to do to me? Hey, Reda, why don't you just change your mind and not do it after all?

Reda: The point is, I've already started it so I can't stop now. I knew that if I talked to you before I did it I'd never do it, so I got Dave to help me.

Jan: If only we knew each other less, you would never be able to do anything to me.

Reda: Aw Jan, life would be no fun at all if I didn't know you so well. You gotta agree! *(They both laugh)*

(The door opens and the teacher, Mr Redford, and Dave enter. The class quietens a little.)

Jan: We will carry on this conversation later.

Reda: Maybe later *you* won't be talking to me!

Jan: And how do you work that one out, Reda? I'm perfectly willing to talk to you.

Mr R: Janice, will you please be quiet. You know perfectly well that there is always silence while I take the register.

Jan: *(Whispered)* To think we all used to drool over him!

Reda: He is such a snide, and he thinks that everyone still fancies him — he always walks around with that smarmy 'cat's got the cream' look on his face.

Jan: You can say that again. To think . . .

Mr R: Janice, I have already told you about talking during registration. And, Janice, what is the meaning of this card from you in my register?

Jan: *(Getting back at him)* It is the class's register, sir. And what card are you talking about?

Mr R: Janice, stop this now! If you cannot explain this card immediately, I will read it out to the rest of the class.

Jan: *(Sincere)* Honestly, sir, I do not know what you are talking about.

Mr R: All right, Janice. You insist on being flippant. I hope a little piece of humiliation will teach you your lesson. The card says, 'Dear, darling, my sweetheart, my honeybunch, it is your anniversary so, as you know, our love is inescapable.' Should I continue?

(The class react with loud hoots and whistles)

Jan: *(Very quietly)* No, sir.

Mr R: Very well. I will not read out any more, but if you continue to insist that you know nothing about it you will get one hour's detention every night this week.

Jan: I do not know anything about the card, sir! I did not write it and I do not know who did, and I do not think it is fair that you should give me detention for something I did not do. It is not fair!

Mr R: The matter is closed, Janice. Make sure you come to detention from tonight. Class dismissed. *(Exit Mr Redford)*

Allen: Hey, Jan darling, I didn't know you were sweet on ol' Mr Sour Grapes Redford. You sure been keeping it to yourself, sugar!

Jan: Shut up, Allen. *REDA*, I could kill you! *(Slowly she begins to laugh)* But did you hear the self-righteous way he read it out? Dave, you and Mike must have composed that lovely piece which has landed me in it.

Dave: At least you recognise genius when you hear it.

Mike: *(To Jan)* 'My sweetheart, my honeybunch' — it is just the sort of thing you would write. I loved it, especially when you were so meek, even when you said that you didn't think it was fair. It was brilliant.

Jan: Well, now I know that I have NO friends, I think it is time I departed to my lesson.

Reda: Hey, Jan, don't go off like that.

Jan: Why not? At this moment in time I could wring your neck! Honestly, with friends like you lot, I don't need enemies. *(She starts to exit)*

Mike: I know the feeling, my sweetheart. *(He is teasing her)*

Jan: Shut up! *(They exit)*

4 *The classroom the next morning*

Jan: Morning, Reda, and how are you this morning?

Reda: I'm fine.

Jan: You know it's my birthday on Saturday?

Reda: You needn't worry, I've already got you a present. And after you were so good about what we did to you yesterday, Dave, Allen and Mike have each bought you one as well.

Jan: Well I expected that, but I wasn't going to remind *you* to get me a present.

Reda: No?

Jan: No! I was going to tell you that I am going to have a party on Saturday.

Reda: Have you got invitation cards?

Jan: Of course. Here is yours.

Reda: Thanks.

(The bell for registration goes)

Jan: Hey, Reda, will you give Dave, Mike and Allen their invites, please? Redford will be here soon, and I have just about had as much of him as I can take.

Reda: I can't, after yesterday. I mean, every time I get anywhere near Dave they just start, so we decided that we would carry on at school as if we weren't going out with each other. I mean, if I were to walk up and give him the invitation they would think it was a love letter or something. Anyway, if you just pop over there now you'll be able to give it to them before old sourface Redford gets here.

Jan: Okay, Reda. *(Meaning she thinks Reda ought to do it)*

Reda: Jan, I can't, it embarrasses me and Dave when they start.

Jan: Okay. *(She moves to the other side of the classroom where the three boys are)*

Allen: Jan, how you doing?

Jan: Fine, Allen.

Dave: Morning, Jan.

Jan: Good morning.

Mike: Good morning, Jan. Why is it that Reda is not over here with you? *(Sarcastic)* After all, there was a time when the two of you were inseparable.

Jan: Shut up, Mike. I have got something to give you three.

Allen: Hey, this sure sounds 'innerestin'. We could be on to something good here.

Mike: Shut up, Allen. What is it that you have got for us, Jan?

Jan: Well, you know that it is my birthday on Saturday?

Mike: Yes, so what? I suppose you know we have already got you presents?

Jan: Actually, I only came over to give you your invitations.

Allen:
Dave: Invitations?
Mike:

Jan: Yes.

Mike: Invitations to what?

(Enter Mr Redford)

Mr R: Good morning, class. Get to your places quickly, please.

Jan: Look, here you are! Quickly – take them.

Mr R: Janice, do you never learn? Will you get to your seat immediately.

Jan: *(Very sharp)* Yes, sir.

Mr R: Just a minute, Janice. What have you just given out?

Jan: Nothing dangerous, sir.

Mr R: Will you stop this impudence, Janice, and tell me what is in the letter you have given out. *(Janice stays silent)* Allen, give me the note Janice gave you.

Allen: Yes, sir. *(He gives him the note)*

Mr R: *(A few moments of mumbling)* Ah, an invitation to your party on Saturday, Janice.

Jan: Yes, sir. Do you want one?

Mr R: I'd have thought you'd already posted it.

Jan: I have, I have. You should get it eventually, sir.

Mr R: *(Outraged)* Janice! Get out of the classroom at once and wait outside!

Jan: Yes, sir. *(Exit)*

(Mr Redford marks the register in silence – there are only a few names left – and then exits. Jan re-enters.)

Mike: Jan, you seem to be making a habit of getting his back up!

Jan: Don't! God, that was so embarrassing!

Allen: It was funny.

Dave: I haven't seen a teacher do that since the infants.

Jan: I thought it was only middle-aged teachers who did things like that.

Reda: You can say that again. But your face was probably born old.

5 *In Jan's house. There is a party going on in the back-ground.*

Mike: Do you want to dance, Jan?

Jan: Yes, okay. *(She doesn't move)*

Mike: Well, come on, then.

Jan: What! Are you asking?

Mike: I'm asking.

Jan: Okay. I'm dancing. *(And now she is — pleased to have teased him)*

Mike: That's better.

Jan: It is?

Mike: Yes. I quite like dancing with you.

Jan: You do?

Mike: Of course.

Dave and Reda: Can we butt in?

Mike: No, buzz off! I'm trying to have a PRIVATE CONVERSATION here.

Dave: Come on, Mike, you must have done all the talking you're gonna do tonight.

Mike: Buzz off, Dave.

Reda: Jan, your mum says she wants to cut the cake and get your presents open after the next record, okay?

Jan: I know, all the lights are coming up after this record.

Reda: Come on, Dave. Can't you tell when we're not wanted?

Dave: Okay.

Mike: Good. Now that they have gone, we can have our private conversation.

Jan: And what are we going to have this discussion on, may I ask?

Mike: I wanted to ask you something.

Jan: You did?

Mike: What I really wanted to know was if you would like to go out with me.

Jan: Well, maybe.

Mike: Jan?

Jan: Yes, of course I want to go out with you.

(The record finishes and the room quietens down)

Jan: Okay, folks, now is the moment you have all been waiting for.

Allen: Oh yeah Jan?

Jan: Of course, Allen. You all get to watch me blowing out my candles and opening the presents you have been so kind as to give me.

Reda: Here's the cake, Jan. You had better hurry, the candles are already lit.

Jan: Okay, here goes.

Dave: Make a wish.

Mike: She's got everything she needs.

(Jan blows out the candles on the cake, then starts to open the presents)

Allen: So the girl has everything she wants, eh Mike?

Reda: Jan, you've left Mike's prezzie for last. Why? That is the question I have to ask. Could it be that you fancy Mike?

Mike: Honestly, Reda, I should hope so. I mean, she is going out with me now!

Reda: Oh.

Jan: Allen, put on another record, please.

Allen: Sure thing. Come on folks, it's time to put on them 'Boogie Shoes' with K.C. and the Sunshine Band. *(The music resumes)*

Jan: Honestly, Reda, you must learn to keep your mouth shut until I have told you all there is to tell.

Reda: Dear Jan, next time I look as if I am going to make a fool of myself, shut me up.

Jan: Absolutely.

Dave: Unless I get there first.

Reda: So why didn't you stop me then?

Mike: Because he did not know.

Jan: It serves you right. You just don't know when to keep your mouth shut; you just seem to have gained the knack of embarrassing me wherever we go.

Reda: I know. But I do try to do it with style!

(Blackout/curtain as another record starts playing)

I Tell a Lie

by Michael Maynard

Cast:
    Alan
    Mothers and Fathers with Babies
    Young Alan
    Mum
    Auntie Doris
    Boy
    Girl
    Market Trader
    Man and Two Women in Advert
    Dog
    Politicians A, B and C
    Dave
    Joy

For a performance of this play, the cast are on stage at all times. They grab appropriate props and costumes when necessary and leap into the acting area. The idea is that Alan talks to the audience and creates a world in order to illustrate his points. The other actors act out the scenes described by him.

Alan: *(To audience)* Hi, Clint Redford's the name. Film star. Well, no, I tell a lie, it isn't actually. It's Alan Roberts. But I am a film star. Soon. Y'see, I finished a film last week. I get it back from the chemist tomorrow! No, seriously, I do actually have in my pocket here . . . a spider. No, really, I have. Wanna see it? You don't believe me, do you? *(Ad lib with the audience)* Why? Don't you trust me? But I tell the truth all the time. And if you believe that, you'll believe anything. But I'm not the only one. You lot tell lies all the time. Yes you do. There's lies everywhere. I'll give you a for-instance. Ever been to a hospital? Maternity ward?

(The other actors divide into babies and parents and they react to Alan's description)

Row after row of new-born babies. Know what I mean? Lying there . . . real ugly-looking mites. Wrinkled like prunes. Sprouting great clumps of hair or bald as a conker. *(The parents faces turn to horror)* Skin all blotchy and horrible. Cross-eyed and mucky nappies. Re-volting! And what do their parents say?

Parents: *(Snapping out of their expressions of horror into ones of delight)* Who's a beautiful baby then? Who's a hand-some/lovely boy/girl. Isn't she/he gorgeous. Isn't she/he wonderful. Oochy coochy coo. Be-ooootiful!

Alan: *(To the actors)* Thank you, thank you. *(They break the scene and go back to their places)* See what I mean? All in the eye of the beholder? P'raps. Maybe they are only lying to themselves. Either way it is stretching the truth a bit. Y'see, I reckon I was destined to lead a life of deception right from the word go. I mean, like most people I was trained for it from an early age. Trained by . . . guess who . . . parents! You must know what I mean. I'll show you. *(An actor comes forward. Alan points at him.)* Me. *(The actor gets down on his knees)* When I was nine years old. My birthday, it was.

(From now on young Alan is called Al. Alan can talk to him and to the audience while the scene is going on. Those in the scene are unaware of his asides.)

Mum: *(Calling)* Alan, Alan, your Auntie Doris'll be here in a minute.

Alan: *(To audience)* Ooh, I hated my Auntie Doris.

Al: Coming, Mum.

Alan: Good little boy, wasn't I?

Mum: Look at you. Just 'cos it's your birthday doesn't mean you can't wash behind your ears.

Al: I did, Mum. Look. Proof. You can see the line where I left off!

Alan: I always had a good sense of humour.

Mum: Make an effort. You only see your auntie once a year . . .

Alan: That was once too often.

Mum: She always comes and gives you a nice present.

Al: Nice?! They're horrible. Never what I want. Like when she bought me an exercise book for my fifth birthday. She's got no idea.

Alan: You can say that again.

Al: No idea.

Alan: *(To Al)* Thank you.

Mum: She was encouraging you . . . starting school and all.

Al: Why can't she get me football boots or a construction kit or something? I bet it'll be a pen like last year or some graph paper. She's always buying me things to make me work harder.

Mum: They're good for you. You be grateful, whatever it is. You ought to be pleased she gives you anything.

Alan: What? Like the time she gave me a clip round the ear.

(Auntie Doris rings the door bell)

Mum: Oh, there she is. Now, whatever you do, don't be rude.

Al: I won't. As long as it's not a set square, or protractor . . .

Alan: Not to mention a compass.

Al: . . . or a compass.

Alan: I told you not to mention a compass!

Mum: Hello, Doris.

Doris: Hello, Edie love. Where's the birthday boy then? Oooh, here he is. Hello, Alan, come and give your auntie a kiss.

Mum: Alan.

Al: Yes, Mum. *(He kisses Doris)*

Alan: Ugh!

Doris: Now look what I've got for you. A present.

Alan: Oh, no.

Al: *(Unenthusiastically)* Oh, thanks.

Doris: Aren't you going to open it? I bet you're excited to know what it is.

Alan: I wouldn't put money on it.

Al: Umm, yes, all right. *(He opens the present)*

Doris: *(While he's opening it)* I always have a good think about what to get you. Boys of today get so many

frivolous, useless things, don't they? I always look for
something useful . . .

Al: Oh . . .

Alan: Help.

Al: A geometry set.

Alan: Oh, no.

Doris: Well, what do you think?

Mum: Come on Alan, thank your auntie.

Al: *(Reluctant)* Auntie . . .

Al and Alan: It's just what I wanted.

Al: I really needed a geometry set. Oh, thank you.

Alan: *(To Al)* Creep.

Doris: That's what I like about you, Alan, you're always so
appreciative.

(The actors break the scene and sit down)

Alan: *(To audience)* See what I mean? If I'd have told the truth
I'd have got a right good hiding. As it was, I was little Lord
Perfect. Still, it's only 'teeny-weeny' white lies, 'cos I don't
want to upset people. Like, I bet you've had a time when
someone knocks at the door . . .

(Boy knocks at a door. Girl answers it.)

. . . and says . . .

Boy: Fancy coming out?

Alan: Now, she can't stand him, right. She hates him. He
repulses her. She wouldn't go out with him if he was the
last person on earth. But what does she say?

Girl: Oh, I'm sorry, I can't. I've got homework to do, and
besides I've got to stay in and look after my brother.

Alan: You see? *(The actors sit down)* But it's not just little white lies that people tell, is it? I mean, some people get away with fibbing all the time.

Market Trader: *(He should be carrying some useless plastic thing)* Listen 'ere, listen 'ere. Now this is good. This is the best. Absolutely unbreakable. Unbreakable. You can drop it, hit it, bang it, thump it, tread on it, drop it from a roof-top, throw it at the wall, hit your granny over the head with it, bash it with a hammer . . . do what you like, you will not break it. Guaranteed!

Alan: You get it home. Breathe on it. And it's in bits all over the floor. The only guarantee you've got is that you can't believe a word they say. And what about those ads on the telly? You know the sort of things. . .

(An acted-out TV commercial. Nice if it could have a musical accompaniment.)

Man: *(Dabbing on aftershave)* 'Butch' . . . the man-size after- shave. Women who inhale the intoxicating aroma will fall at your feet. . . .

Two Women: *(They mime stroking and grabbing him, perhaps from a slight distance)* Oooooh darling. . . . Mmmmm, I just love that strange sensation. . . . Mmm.

Man: If you don't want to try too hard, then the next time, after a close shave, be a man . . . splash on some 'Butch'.

All Three: Probably the most desired aftershave in the world! *(The actors sit down)*

Alan: I bought some of that stuff. *(He mimes splashing it on . . . face, under the arms, everywhere. He starts acting 'Butch'. Walking past the other actors. . . .)* I'd walk into a room and people would say . . .

Actors: *(Each taking a different sentence or improvising equivalent)* There's a funny pong in 'ere. What's that smell? Open a window, quick. *(Their reaction grows until they're all choking and holding their noses)*

Alan: All right, all right! *(They stop)* Mind you, even my dog wouldn't come walkies with me. *(Calling dog)* Here, Rover. *(Actor playing dog comes over, sniffs, rolls over dead, on its back with legs in the air.)* You see. They get away with it. Stretching the truth a bit. No wonder I'm like I am. Ah, but 'It's bound to happen when people are selling things,' I hear you say, 'It's only natural. You don't get respectable people behaving like that.' Wanna bet? How about the people who run the country? Politicians.

(Three politicians come forward wearing huge rosettes with 'Vote for me' on them)

These people never tell lies, do they? The odd 'terminal logical inexactitude', perhaps . . . but never lies . . .

Politician A: Vote for me for a better future . . .

Politician B: Vote for me for a better tomorrow . . .

Politician C: Vote for me for a better life . . .

A: Vote for me because under our control, organisation will be more efficient and we can reach our goals . . .

B: Vote for me because under our control the mechanics of government will work for the people and we can realise all our aspirations . . .

C: Vote for me because together we can achieve all our ideals and march proudly into the promised land . . .

A: I promise you a new age of prosperity.

B: I promise you a new free society; free from the shackles of hardship.

C: I promise you a new beginning, where the wealth of the nation will be harnessed to serve you all.

A, B and C: WE PROMISE!

Alan: However . . . No sooner do they get into power and are in a position to keep their promises, than what do we find . . . ?

(The politicians take off their rosettes. Their smiles disappear.)

A: You see, circumstances change . . .

B: The seriousness of our economic situation . . .

C: The realities of the pressures upon us . . .

(Alan tries to act out their instructions — echoing their words as he does so.)

A: You must sit tight, and yet stand firm . . .

(Someone brings Alan a chair)

Alan: Sit tight . . . stand firm . . . *[etc.]*

B: Walking the tightrope of political options . . .

C: With your feet placed firmly on the ground . . .

A: With your backs to the wall, you must stand up and be counted.

B: And walk tall, whilst of course maintaining a low profile.

C: It's no good sitting on the fence, you must tighten your belts, in order to balance the books.

(Someone gives Alan a pile of books)

A: Roll up your sleeves . . .

B: Pull up your socks . . .

C: Square your shoulders . . .

A, B and C: And TAKE THE MEDICINE.

Alan: *(Does so)* Ugh! But, hang on, hang on! What about prosperity, the new beginning, the new future?

A: Ah . . . well . . .

Alan: What about the promised land?

B: Promises are always conditional.

(The politicians walk off muttering in agreement about how difficult their jobs are)

Alan: Words, words. Funny, no matter how many long words they use, it still sounds like lying to me. Now if the people at the top mislead others, is it any wonder I caught the habit. But with me it's harmless fun. . . . Exaggerating, fantasising. I get right carried away sometimes. Oooh, it's great.

(Joy and David, two of Alan's friends take up their positions in a coffee bar. Alan joins them.)

Joy: Hello, Alan . . . how're you then?

Alan: Oh, a bit fed up really.

Dave: Why, what's up?

Alan: They're always bugging me for information.

Joy: What d'you mean?

Alan: Well, advice really. They don't 'bug' me in fact . . . they normally just ask.

Joy: Who do?

Dave: What are you talking about?

Alan: The Government.

Joy: Which government?

Alan: Ours. Well, one particular department anyway.

Dave: Oh. Which one?

Alan: The Secret Service.

Dave: WHAT!?

Joy: Why do they want you?

Alan: Well, I've been involved in certain activities for them in the past.

Joy: What, like 'spying'?

Alan: Well, I wouldn't say that . . .

Dave: No, I bet you wouldn't.

Alan: I'd say 'undercover surveillance operations'.

Joy: Wow!

Alan: Only a bit. You know, whilst I'm on my travels.

Dave: You mean that time you went off for a month?

Alan: One of them, yes.

Joy: How did you get involved?

Alan: Well, it was after I learnt to sail.

Dave: I didn't know you could.

Alan: A bit, yes. So, crossing borders and frontiers comes easy, see.

Joy: Suppose so. In a boat.

Alan: Particularly sailing round the world.

Dave: What?

Alan: In that race, you know? I didn't win though.

Dave: No, I bet.

Alan: I had to stop.

Dave: Still, must have been great having a go.

Alan: I reckon I could have won, though. But we hit this storm, see. Twenty-foot waves, gale-force winds, water lashing my face; you could hardly stand up. . . .

Joy: Must've been really frightening.

Alan: It was for the crew of the boat that capsized. If we hadn't got them out of the water instantly, they'd be dead now.

Joy: Amazing.

Alan: Still it all turned out okay in the end.

(Joy and Dave are beginning to get suspicious now)

Dave: Great.

Alan: Yeah, funny coincidence really. You see, they were in the music business — the guys we saved.

Dave: Oh, what did they play?

Alan: No, they made records . . . produced them and things. And they were in a bit of a fix. They'd booked a studio to cut a new album and the lead singer in this band had backed out.

Dave: *(Sarcastic)* They could've got me. I'd have done it.

Alan: No, you see, they heard me singing on deck one night, and that was it. They begged me to do it.

Joy: You?

Alan: Yeah.

Joy: But you can't sing.

Alan: Wait till you hear the album.

Dave: Give over.

Alan: Straight up. I just managed to fit it in after the trial for United.

Joy: WHAT!?

Dave: You had a trial for United?

Alan: They kept it quiet, of course, so as not to upset the other players, but they wanted to put me straight in the first team.

Dave: Oh, yeah.

Joy: Come off it, Alan.

Alan: They're waiting till they get to the final. Then they're going to play me as their surprise secret weapon.

Dave: *(Trying to annoy)* You mean like 'playing their joker'!?

Joy: *(Indignant)* Playing their liar, more like it!

Alan: You'll see. You'll see!

(Joy and Dave freeze)

Alan: *(To audience)* You see . . . *(Not so confident now)* it impresses people.

The Whole Cast: *(Not impressed)* WOW! *(Joy and Dave go and sit back with the others)*

Alan: Anyway, I'm nearing the end of my little journey through the world of deceit. But here's the best bit. Ah yes, you'll like this. It's great.

(He's a bit desperate. The cast show just a flicker of excitement.)

It's the scene where . . . No, I tell a lie . . . It's the end. *(Groans of disappointment from the rest of the cast)* Oh, and by the way, knowing what a liar I am . . . Can you believe anything I've said? But then . . . *(Looks round audience)* it takes one to know one, doesn't it. See ya!

Hands Off!

by Marianne Cook

Cast: TV Film Crew: Director, Sound Technician,
            Cameraman, Director's Assistant
         Mike, TV presenter
         Mrs Evans, an old lady
         Mr Evans, her husband
         Inspector, chairman of the public enquiry
         Secretary
         Mr Grainger, Electricity Board representative
         Mr Sealy, environment spokesman
         Hecklers, at the public enquiry
         Lizzy Price, teenage girl
         Mrs Price, her mum
         Mr Price, her dad, a shepherd
         Hugh Pugh, a modern Noah
         Two Boys
         Post-mistress
         Two Policemen
         Neighbour

1 *Outside a chapel. A TV film crew are preparing a documentary programme. Mike stands, ready and eager, microphone in hand, in front of the chapel doors. The Director's assistant is between Mike and the camera, waiting to 'mark' the take. From inside the chapel, the small congregation can be heard singing, 'God works in a mysterious way, his wonders to perform'.*

Director: Ready on sound?

Sound Technician: Ready.

Director: Ready, camera?

Cameraman: Ready.

Director: Ready, Mike?

Mike: And waiting.

Director: Mark it.

Assistant: *(Holding up clapperboard) The World Before Us,* Aberfenny, Take Four. *(He moves out of camera line)*

Director: Go.

Mike: *(Enthusiastically)* Here, in the tiny village of Aberfenny in Mid-Wales, God does indeed work in a mysterious way, his wonders to perform. God . . . and the Electricity Board. For if their plans go ahead as they intend, this delightful rural peace will be swept away by millions of gallons of water. In future, the chapel bell will be heard, like the bell of Atlantis in the fables of old, from under the waves. *(He moves to one side of the chapel, where the view behind him takes in the site of the planned hydro-electric scheme)* Hydro-electric power is the name of the game. Power for industry across the border in England. Some say the new dam will be a great achievement. Magnificent! Awe-inspiring! But what about the villagers of Aberfenny, who will lose their homes when the valley is flooded? Do they feel the same? That's what I'm here on this quiet Sunday evening to try and find out.

Director: Cut.

2 *Outside the chapel, a little later. The singing has stopped. The service is finished. Mike is waiting to talk to people as they leave. The crew are ready to film.*

Director: Keep your eyes skinned for the old lady in the blue velvet hat.

Mike: Will do.

Director: I've heard she's quite a character. Ready, Mike?

Mike: And waiting. *(The chapel doors are thrown open)*

Director: Ready everyone. Here they come!

(The congregation begin to come out of the chapel. Mike watches for the lady in the blue hat, and when he sees her, he steps forward and thrusts the microphone under her nose.)

Mike: Mrs Evans? It is Mrs Evans, isn't it?

Mrs Evans: *(Suspicious)* And if it is?

Mike: Mrs Evans, as the oldest inhabitant of Aberfenny . . . how old is it exactly?

Mrs E: What's my age got to do with you? Mind your own business, young man.

Mike: *(Carrying on regardless)* What do you think of the plan to flood your village?

Mrs E: Not much.

Mike: Where will you and your husband go from here?

Mrs E: Who said we're going anywhere?

Mike: Your cottage will be thirty foot under water. Have the council offered you a place in an old people's home?

Mrs E: What do we want with an old people's home? We can look after ourselves.

Mike: A flat, then?

Mrs E: They might have made an offer. There was a letter. But we haven't got around to reading it yet.

Mike: They *do* care then, what becomes of you?

Mrs E: How should I know, if they care or not? Why don't you ask them?

Mike: Well, yes . . . perhaps . . .

Mrs E: Good at asking questions, aren't you? Harpies you are, feeding on the misfortunes of others.

Mike: No, Mrs Evans. We really do care, even if the council . . .

Mrs E: *(Interrupts him sharply)* Care! All you care about is your programme.

Mike: Thank you very much, Mrs Evans.

Director: *(Quickly)* Cut!

3 *Mr and Mrs Evans' cottage, two weeks later. Mr and Mrs Evans have been watching* The World Before Us. *As the interview she gave ends, Mrs Evans gets up and switches off the TV set. She is very pleased with her performance.*

Mrs E: He didn't half bundle me along fast there! But I showed him. I didn't think they'd leave that bit in. Speechless, he was.

Mr E: You were very good.

Mrs E: You should have been at chapel. You could have been in it too.

Mr E: No need. You said everything that needed to be said.

Mrs E: That's true.

Mr E: And now we've done with saying things.

Mrs E: What do you mean?

Mr E: Now . . . it's time for doing things. Time for action.

Mrs E: What can we do? Against them. If they've made up their minds.

Mr E: There's going to be a public enquiry.

Mrs E: That's just more talk.

Mr E: Well, I'm going to go anyhow. You can give up and stay at home if you like.

Mrs E: Who said anything about giving up?

4 *Inside the village hall. The hall is crowded with villagers angrily protesting against the Electricity Board's plan. On the platform sit the Inspector, who is chairman of the meeting, and a secretary, taking notes. Mr Grainger, the Electricity Board representative, is trying to make himself heard above the voices.*

Mr G: We have tried to check the demand for power. But at peak times, people want more electricity than we can supply.

Heckler: Let them want!

Another Heckler: Let their homes be flooded!

Third Heckler: Why should we be the ones to suffer!

Mr G: We have to find a way of making more electricity.

(The noise becomes overwhelming)

Inspector: *(Banging on the table)* Ladies and gentlemen . . . Please . . . You must give Mr Grainger a fair hearing. Your turn will come later. *(The heckling continues)* If you aren't quiet, I will have to have the hall cleared. *(The voices quieten down a little)* Thank you. Mr Grainger?

Mr G: You talk about suffering. Well, this isn't a perfect world. We have to measure suffering against suffering. In this village a few people will lose their homes if this plan goes ahead. If it doesn't, next winter we shall have more power cuts. Many old people will suffer. Sick people. Industry will suffer. Still more people will lose their jobs. I'm sorry about your village.

Hecklers: Get away . . . Pull the other one . . . Shame!

Mr G: I am sorry . . . but a choice must be made. You can't make an omelette without breaking eggs . . .

Heckler: Tell that to the eggs! *(Cheers from audience)*

Inspector: I've warned you . . . *(The cheers become an uproar)* Clear the hall! Clear the hall!

5 *Inside the village hall, later. The loudest protesters have been removed. The enquiry continues more peacefully. Mr Grainger sits on the platform. Mr Sealy gets up to address the audience.*

Inspector: Mr David Sealy is going to speak for the 'Friends of the Environment'.

Mr S: I won't take up much of your time. Mr Grainger's dam will, no doubt, be a grand sight. A wonder of science. This valley will become a beautiful lake. People will be able to sail on it. To fish in it.

Mr G: Indeed. A great attraction.

Mr S: But . . . what will be lost? This valley, I grant you, is not unique. But what we do have here are hedgerows and meadows that have taken centuries to evolve. Here is a place where people live in harmony with nature. Such places are rare. They should not be trampled by the march of so-called progress.

Audience: Hear, hear! That's right . . . Good point . . . *(Some clapping)*

Mr S: Mr Grainger argues that his scheme is necessary to produce more power. I say to him there are other ways of producing that power. There is energy in the wind, in the sun and in the waves . . .

Mr G: *(Interrupts)* They're not economic.

Mr S: How do you know? We haven't even begun to look into them properly. I repeat, we have the wind, the sun and the waves. We don't have to destroy the life of this valley and its people.

(The audience applaud Mr Sealy. He sits down, pleased.)

Inspector: Thank you, Mr Sealy.

Mr Evans: *(Gets up from his seat near the back of the hall)* Mr Inspector, sir. . . .

Inspector: Who is it?

Mr E: Albert Evans, sir. Parish councillor. May I have a word?

Inspector: Keep it short, Mr Evans.

Mr E: I will. I'm not a clever man. I haven't any clever arguments like Mr Grainger and Mr Sealy. All I want to say is this.

Mr G: *(Mutters)* Get on with it.

Mr E: I'm 81 years old. My wife, Annie, is 86. We've lived here, both of us, all our lives. We've got our roots here, and roots are important. We don't want to be pulled up like a couple of cabbages and moved somewhere else at our time of life. *(Agreement from the audience)* If people matter, like Mr Grainger said, if suffering matters, well then *we're* people and, God help us, *our* suffering matters too.

(Audience applauds)

6 *The Prices' cottage. Lizzy Price and her mother are sprawled at the kitchen table, enjoying a cup of tea.*

Mrs P: Your dad says the Inspector's going to find for the Electric.

Lizzy: How long will it take them to build the dam?

Mrs P: Not long. When they want something that bad, they know how to get on with it.

Lizzy: We'll be moving soon, then.

Mrs P: I reckon . . . *(Her dream seems about to come true)* A nice council flat in the town . . .

Lizzy: I won't have to spend hours every day on the bus. We'll be just round the corner from the school.

Mrs P: Central heating . . . no more humping old coal.

Lizzy: Two cinemas, with two films each every week . . . not just the village hall with three films a year, and all as old as geography textbooks.

Mrs P: A half-tiled bathroom with separate toilet. Constant hot water and a matching pampas suite.

Lizzy: Discos four times a week with visiting live acts, and talent-spotting competitions on Saturday nights.

Mrs P: A fully-fitted kitchen . . .

Lizzy: Cafés that stay open till twelve o'clock at night . . .

Mrs P: Carpets you can sink into . . .

(Mr Price comes in quietly. He stands and listens.)

Lizzy: The chance to have a good time . . .

Mrs P: A bit of luxury . . .

Lizzy: Lots of young people . . .

Mrs P: All mod cons . . .

Lizzy: Boys . . .

Mrs P: Launderettes . . .

Lizzy: Living it up . . .

Mr Price: *(Not able to stand it any longer)* But no life!

(Mrs Price and Lizzy jump)

Lizzy: Dad!

Mr P: I've told you before, I'm not going to rot in that stinking town.

Mrs P: And I'm not going to rot in this dump of a village when I don't have to.

Mr P: Mr Jenkins, over in the next valley, he's looking for a shepherd. I'll get a good reference. I only lost three lambs this year.

Mrs P: You've been offered a job at the smelting works.

Mr P: I don't have to take it. I'm a free man.

Mrs P: But what about us? What about Lizzy and me?

Mr P: There's a cottage goes with the position.

Mrs P: Another old shack like this, I suppose?

Mr P: You could come and look at it. I'm going to see Mr Jenkins this evening.

Mrs P: No point. We've made up our minds. Lizzy and me are moving to the town.

Lizzy: Yes, Dad. We want a bit of life.

Mr P: *(With feeling)* How can you call it life? You've held in your arms the scrap of a lamb I dug out of the snow. You've warmed it, and made it breathe again when it was all but dead. That's life, girl. Not discos and cafés and cinemas. They're just the scum that's floated to the top.

7 *The lane that runs beside Pugh's garden. Hidden beyond the fence, Pugh is hammering. Two boys, at a loss for something to do, are ambling along the lane, trying to trip each other up. They are stopped in their tracks by Pugh, who declaims at the top of his voice, still unseen.*

Pugh: The earth also was corrupt before God and was filled with violence. *(Sound of hammering replaced by sound of sawing)*

First Boy: What's old Pugh doing in his back garden?

Second Boy: Haven't you heard? He's building an ark. To save him from the flood.

First Boy: I don't believe it.

Second Boy: I'm telling you he is. Mad as a hatter!

(Pugh's head appears above the fence)

Pugh: What are you boys doing behind my fence?

First Boy: Nothing. *(The boys giggle)*

Pugh: *(A little more of him appears above the fence. He brandishes a saw.)* Nothing? Boys are always up to something. Some wickedness or other.

Second Boy: Is it true, what they're saying, Hugh Pugh?

Pugh: That depends what it is they are saying, doesn't it, boy?

Second Boy: They say you're building an ark.

Pugh: And what is it to them if I am? *(He strains higher. He is not very securely balanced.)* And God said unto Noah, make thee an ark of gopher wood. I will destroy the whole earth. *(He topples over and disappears behind the fence again)*

First Boy: It's not God. It's the Electricity Company, and they're only going to flood the valley.

Pugh: *(Poking his head over the fence)* That's what they tell you.

(He returns to his work)

Second Boy: Noah was millions of years ago.

Pugh: The truth of God's holy book is like a stream that is constantly renewed.

First Boy: *(Climbing on the fence)* What are you going to put into your ark, Hugh Pugh?

Pugh: Mr Pugh, if you don't mind.

Second Boy: *(Joining his friend on the fence)* Dogs and cats?

First Boy: Cows and goats?

Second Boy: Lions and tigers?

First Boy: Kangaroos?

Second Boy: Elephants?

First Boy: Not many elephants in Aberfenny.

Boys: *(Sing)* The animals went in two by two . . . *[etc.]*

Pugh: *(Turning on them)* Stop it! Get off my fence! Be off with you! Go on! *(The boys get down, laughing, and go, still singing)* Unbelievers! Behold! I, even I, do bring a flood of water upon the earth, to destroy all flesh. *(There is a crash of thunder and it begins to rain)* Oh no, God. Not yet. *(Pugh pulls his jacket over his head)* I haven't got the roof on yet. No . . .

8 *The village shop and sub-post office, some time later. The post-mistress is behind the counter. The bell over the shop door rings as Mrs Evans comes in. She has a lot on her mind.*

Post-mistress: Good morning, Mrs Evans.

Mrs E: There's not a lot good about it I can see.

Post-mistress: Come for your pension, have you?

Mrs E: I want the money from my post office account.

Post-mistress: Let's do the pension first . . . *(She takes the book)* Did you see in the paper, those TV people are coming back again? To film the opening of the dam? Pity you won't be here to give them another interview. *(She counts out the money)*

Mrs E: Maybe I will and maybe I won't.

Post-mistress: What's that? *(Mrs Evans glares at her)* Sorry, dear, I was counting.

Mrs E: *(Thrusts her post office book across the counter)* Twenty-two pounds, fifty-three pence. All of it.

Post-mistress: You don't have to draw it all out, dear. Just because this office is closing.

Mrs E: I want it, just the same. And then I've got a grocery order for you, the other side. *(She means the other side of the small shop)*

Post-mistress: *(Concentrating on the money)* The usual bits and pieces, I expect.

Mrs E: I've made a list. *(She begins to read it, quite fast)* Six pounds of self-raising . . . twenty pounds of potatoes . . . three jars of coffee . . . two pounds of tea . . . four packets of digestives . . . large tin of cocoa . . . two pounds of butter, two of marg . . . six tins of vegetable soup . . . .

Post-mistress: What are you going to do with all that?

Mrs E: What do you think I'm going to do with it?

Post-mistress: But so much . . . How are you going to carry it all home?

Mrs E: My Albert's outside with the wheelbarrow. *(The post-mistress is silenced)* Just you put it up and be quick. All right?

9 *The front garden of the Evans' cottage. Mr Evans is on a step-ladder, nailing planks across the window. Mrs Evans is beside him, handing him nails and steadying the ladder. They are like children with a new game.*

Mrs E: The neighbours will think you're building an ark, like poor old Hugh Pugh.

Mr E: They can think what they like. I don't care. Did you remember to buy candles?

Mrs E: A couple of dozen. It was all she had.

Mr E: They're bound to cut off the electric. And the water. To try and force us out.

Mrs E: I filled up the bath, and two buckets and some pans. That'll last us a good while if we're careful.

Mr E: *(Hammers home the last nail)* There! That's all the windows boarded up. *(Mrs Evans helps him down. He gives her the hammer and folds up the step-ladder.)* We'll go inside and lock and bolt the doors. And push the furniture against them.

Mrs E: Can't that wait till tomorrow? You look worn out.

Mr E: No. There isn't a moment to waste. Come on.

Mrs E: Oh Albert . . . isn't it exciting!

Mr E: Exciting? It's more than exciting! It's the chance I've been waiting for all my life. It's Us against Them! That's what it is!

(They go in. Sound of many bolts and locks.)

10 *The front garden of the Evans' cottage, three days later. Two policemen have been summoned. They are discussing the situation with a neighbour.*

Neighbour: I thought I had to phone you. Three days it's been like this. I know there's something wrong.

First Policeman: *(Examines the planks across the window. They are firmly fixed.)* Another nutter?

Neighbour: Nothing like that.

First Policeman: Windows at the back?

Neighbour: Boarded up, like this one.

First Policeman: Go round and check, Len. *(The second policeman goes round to the back of the cottage)*

Neighbour: They're not nutters. An old couple. Mr and Mrs Evans. Upset about the Electric scheme. Don't want to move out.

First Policeman: How long have they been in there?

Neighbour: I noticed the boards when I came home from work on Monday.

(The second policeman returns)

Second Policeman: All secure at the back. Door's locked as well.

First Policeman: They've been shut in for three days then?

Neighbour: I thought it was funny. Place all closed up, and them not supposed to be going till the weekend.

First Policeman: You are sure they're in there?

Neighbour: Of course I am. I knocked at the door. They didn't answer but I could hear them — whispering. Through the letter-box.

First Policeman: *(Tries the front door. It doesn't budge.)* Do you know who their doctor is?

Neighbour: No . . . Old Doc Davies, I suppose . . . .

First Policeman: Could you find out?

Neighbour: I could ask . . .

First Policeman: Good. We may need him. *(He turns to the second policeman. The neighbour gets the message and goes.)* Evans, did she say the name was?

Second Policeman: Dunno.

First Policeman: Give it a try.

Second Policeman: *(Bangs on the door-knocker and shouts)* Mr Evans . . . Can you hear me, Mr Evans? *(He waits a bit. There is no reply.)* It's the police . . . Will you answer, please? *(He knocks again)*

First Policeman: These old folks can be stubborn when they've a mind to it. Let me try. *(He bends down and speaks through the letter-box. The gentle approach.)* Come on now, Mr and Mrs Evans . . . We want to help you. Get this thing sorted out proper . . . You can't stay here . . . No use getting all upset. You haven't any choice.

Mr E: *(Shouts from inside the cottage)* Oh, haven't I! I'm telling you, you're not going to get me out of my house. Sixty years we've lived here, and we intend to die here, Annie and me.

Mrs E: That's right!

Mr E: Flood the valley! You'll have to drown us in our beds. We're not going nowhere. So hands off! You get your hands . . .

(He breaks down)

Mrs E: Albert . . . Oh . . . no . . . *(Something is very wrong)*

First Policeman: Open the door, Mrs Evans. *(We hear thumps and bumps from inside the cottage. Mrs Evans is trying to move furniture away from the door.)*

Mrs E: I'm trying . . .

Mr E: *(Faint)* Don't let them in, Annie . . .

Mrs E: I got to.

Mr E: No . . .

(The door opens. Mrs Evans is shaking and exhausted. Mr Evans is lying on the floor.)

Mrs E: The doctor said he shouldn't get over-excited.

Mr E: First time in sixty years you ever let me down, Annie.

11 *Outside the chapel. The TV film crew are back.*

Director: Ready on sound?

Sound Technician: Ready.

Director: Ready, camera?

Cameraman: Ready.

Director: Ready, Mike?

Mike: And waiting.

Director: Mark it.

Assistant: *(Holding up clapperboard) The World Before Us*,
Aberfenny Postscript, Take One. *(He moves out of
camera line)*

Director: Go.

Mike: *(Springs into action)* Today, I'm standing for the last
time here in Aberfenny. The village is empty. The people
have gone to new homes and new lives. Tomorrow the
waters will close over the grey stone cottages and the little
white bell tower . . . *(From up the valley, the sound of
a great deal of water roaring slowly nearer, begins to build)*
The sound of children at play will be heard no more . . .

Director: *(Cuts in)* What date did you say they were going to
switch on?

Assistant: The twenty-fourth.

Director: That's today, not tomorrow! *(Screams)* CUT!

(The sound of water is louder . . .)

Mike: What's the matter?

Director: Strike everything! *(The film crew collect their gear
in a panic)*

Mike: What!

Director: Behind you!

Mike: *(Looks round)* Wow!

Director: Come on, everyone! *(The film crew scatter in a big hurry. Mike remains, devoted to duty, always the professional.)*

Mike: As I look towards the head of the valley, a mountain of water towers above me . . . *(A shadow looms over him)*

Director: *(Distant and frenzied)* Mike . . .

Mike: . . . defying the force of gravity. A gigantic and powerful monument to the cleverness of man . . .

(The water roars. Suddenly, all is dark and silent. From out of the darkness, the chapel bell is heard tolling slowly beneath the water.)

Notes to the plays

Listen to the Pin Drop

In real life you expect people to have many different facets
to their personalities. Comedy works by exaggerating one
of the facets of a character out of all proportion to the rest.
In this play, the Rowdies are very rowdy, the Pindrops very
quiet, and Liz and Sonny are the two extremes of
pessimism and optimism.

The result, of course, is conflict, and a serious problem
for the characters involved. From the outside it's funny,
perhaps because we can see a little bit of ourselves in these
characters, and realise that there are days in our lives when
we ourselves become dangerously close to turning into
people like them.

The characters

The characters must be played broadly. Enjoy the exag-
geration, but even so, make sure it is in keeping with the
character's basic attitude. 'Broadness' doesn't mean that
you can add any embellishment whatsoever.

You could spend a little time discussing the relationships. Who is really the boss in the Pindrop household?
Can you ever imagine there being peace in the Rowdies'
home? The Uppendowns are opposites — Liz is always
miserable (a pessimist) and Sonny is always sunny (an
optimist).

In case you think these characters are nothing but
stereotypes or cartoon figures, you might examine the
state of each household at the end of the play and ask
yourself how it has changed from that at the beginning.
On the next day will it all go on the same as before — like
a gramophone record played over and over again — or is
there a glimmer of hope for them?

Movement and gesture are important in comedy and

you should work on the contrasts between the characters. Does Mrs Pindrop ever get out of her chair? Does Mr Pindrop always tiptoe instead of walking? On the whole, would optimists go expansively out to meet the world with open arms, while pessimists go more cautiously, hanging back, and keeping within a smaller circle?

Finally, what do the characters do when the action has moved away from them into one of the other flats?

People who like to classify plays would call one like this a 'comedy of humours', because hundreds of years ago doctors believed that the body contained four important fluids that determined the personality. They were blood, phlegm, choler, and bile or melancholy. If you had too much choler in you, you were choleric — hot-tempered and angry; too much phlegm and you were phlegmatic — sluggish and apathetic; too much blood and you were sanguine — courageous and optimistic; too much bile or melancholy — the phrase still speaks for itself. A quaint and untrue theory, but you may feel that there is still some connection between a person's general physical state and their personality.

Masks

These characters are a bit like characters you may have come across in the *commedia dell' arte* — troupes of Italian actors who improvised plays at the time of Shakespeare. They played their 'type' characters in half-masks, and you could experiment along the same lines, making masks that exaggerate the appropriate facial features. Perhaps Sonny's mask should be large and have an enormous smile; Liz Miz's mask could be small and frowning with worry. What sort of noses should the Pindrops have, and should the Rowdies have ugly faces like the noise they make?

Masks for plays with dialogue must be very light, fit well, especially at the eyes, and allow the voice to be projected outwards. It is not easy to make such masks, but well worth trying. Masks modelled in papier-mâché on clay formers are nearly always unwearable. Here are three methods which are likely to be more successful.

Two methods use one-inch (2.5 cm) gummed brown paper tape. You blow up a balloon to the size of your head, using loops of string to compare circumferences. Then you cover it with tissue paper and several layers of the gummed paper. When this is dry, you let down the balloon and cut out a large 'neck' hole, big enough to get the mask over your head. You slit it and repair it (which is easy with the gummed paper) until it's a comfortable fit, then you cut out eyeholes (eyes are surprisingly close together, and if you guess, you will almost certainly get the distance wrong) and a mouth hole.

Alternatively, instead of a balloon, you can work in pairs on each other. You hold the tissue paper in place over your hair and face, and a friend puts a layer of gummed paper over you. It's best to start with a 'Red Indian' head-band of paper to hold the tissue, and then to build up a skullcap. Finally your friend should start working down the sides of your face and across to the nose, leaving the eyes and mouth till last for obvious reasons.

The third method is to put on a bathing cap, cover the face with a thick layer of petroleum jelly, and use plaster bandages (the sort used for broken arms and legs). To be on the safe side, insert straws in the nostrils to start with. With this method you shouldn't attempt to cover the scalp, only the forehead, cheeks and nose. The bandages must be left to set, and this will only take a few minutes. Of course, it is important not to get your hair trapped in the plaster!

These last two methods should be used under adult supervision and only by responsible students. The masks fit quite tightly, and you need to have some scissors handy so that, if necessary, they can be carefully slit up the back or beneath the nose in order to get them off. If you have any doubts about these two methods, stick to using the balloon as a basis for the mask.

In all three cases, when the masks are adjusted to a good fit (and not before), you can build up exaggerated features and paint them.

Treat the masks with respect — they can have considerable dramatic power. Never put them on except in front of a mirror, and then gaze at your masked self for a

while, letting the mask work its character into you. (The
Japanese Noh theatre actors call this process 'saluting the
mask'.) If you want to be yourself again, take the mask off.
Don't try to be yourself inside the mask. If you don't treat
the mask with ceremony, it will no longer have any effect
on you – or therefore on other people. (There is an
interesting radiovision called 'Masks and Costume' in the
BBC radio series *Theatre Workshop*.)

Staging

You need to mark out roughly square spaces representing
the flats belonging to the three families. The Rowdies'
flat should have a sink and two doorways, one to Nicola's
bedroom and one to the living-room, as well as the front
door opening on to the balcony outside.

The Pindrops' flat could have two matching armchairs,
and you might enjoy 'dressing' the set with precisely
arranged ornaments.

The Uppendowns' flat should look drab, and so should
Liz Miz. The one touch of flamboyant colour could be
Sonny himself.

If you plan to show the play to an audience, then the
flats should be in a line, with the Rowdies to the audience's
right, the Pindrops in the middle and the Uppendowns to
the audience's left. A connecting balcony runs across
between flats and audience.

If you are able to set stage lighting, it will help the play
to cross-fade between the rooms as the action changes.
There should probably always be some light on all of the
flats. You will need to mask spotlights to make square
shapes for the rooms.

Sound effects

Effects are very important to this play. You will need discs
and a record player for Nicola. For the sound effects of the
drill and washing-machine you will probably need to make
your own recordings. You could keep the two sounds on
separate cassettes perhaps, and play them on separate
recorders as a way of mixing them when the play needs it.

Discussion and follow-up

1   What situations do you find comic? How much do they depend on the characters of the people involved?

2   List and discuss as many character 'types' as you can, going for temperament and emotion rather than any physical attributes. (Though physique may help define characters in many traditional comic forms, for example the relative sizes of Laurel and Hardy, or the pretty Cinderella against the Ugly Sisters. Note that the comedy arises from the contrast embodied in the pairings.) Group the 'types' in ways that you feel could lead to comedy and improvise or write scenes around them.

3   Write down jokes, trying to make them seem as funny on the page.

4   Do you think comedy is funny because we feel superior to people in the play? Do we have to recognise some of our failings in order to find a play comic?

5   Although this play is a comedy, the issues it deals with are fundamentally serious. In real life, how do you think a quiet family would cope with living next to a rowdy one?

6   Do you know of friendships (or marriages) between opposites like Liz and Sonny? How much do you feel friendship thrives on sharing the same things, and how much are differences of temperament important so that the friendship does not turn stale?

7   Is it inevitable that one partner must dominate any relationship?

I Could Wring Her Neck

Julia James was seventeen when she wrote this script for
Drama Workshop. The bubbling liveliness of the dialogue
accurately reflects the speech of young people. The
characters too, and the mixture of rivalry and friendliness
they show towards each other, will be familiar to all school
students.

It's not a play that attempts to make earth-shattering
statements. But it has an appealing warmth and accurate
observation of the rapidly shifting currents of teenage
friendships.

The characters

Everyone has experienced a desire to help their best friend,
and like Jan we may not stop to consider whether they do
in fact need our help, nor whether we really have their best
interests at heart. After all, 'doing good' is one of the few
things that can give us a nice warm glow, and the chances
are that no one will notice if we end up self-righteously
indignant when our help is rejected.

Reda no doubt is perfectly capable of looking after
herself, but Jan *needs* to do her a good turn. Mike and
Allen are quick to sense a chance to get their own back on
a girl who is already so much in control that they have
clearly suffered from her tongue in the past. Dave is also
made a fool of, but perhaps it's worth it. He really does
seem to fancy Reda, and the friendship is begun by the
end of the play. Whether it will last in the face of Reda's
storminess is a different matter, but at least he will have
had his chance. Indeed, Reda may well be attracted by his
apparent gentleness.

They all know each other's weak spots ('We know each
other too well') and yet their bickering, and even the
central revenge, isn't spiteful — it simply takes advantage of
the friendship.

Mr Redford has an unenviable task teaching these young people, because any lesson will seem dull in comparison with the rich life they weave for themselves. So far as acting him is concerned, he needs plenty of reaction from the class. He has to fight to keep order against their continuous chattering and bickering. For this reason it's important that there are 'extras' in the classroom besides the named characters. These other students are also needed as 'audience' for Jan, Mike and Allen's game with Reda and Dave.

Apart from these general ideas, when you come to play the parts, look carefully in the script for clues to the kind of person your character is. Even more important, try to look carefully for the clues which tell you when you are riding high on the seesaw of the relationships, and the moment when you've been crashed.

Language

The key to playing this piece is speed. When the first actors met it (they were a youth drama group working with Pat Keysell and Jim Mienzakowski in Peckham) they did a double-take. At first sight, it doesn't seem easy to read. But once you get into it, you will find that the speech rhythms are very strong, and that they will carry you.

One of the difficulties a modern playwright encounters is in finding a way of writing down speech that's close to the everyday. The writer wants to represent a particular dialect or particular intonation, but finds it difficult to translate this into standard spelling and punctuation. One example of the kind of (apparent) problems you will meet is to do with Jan's 'do's' and 'do not's'. You will see that Jan often uses them and they may appear strange on the page. In fact, we quite often unconsciously use this form of speech when we talk, but it only looks odd written down. When you read it, try stressing 'do' rather than 'not': 'I *did* not write it and I *do* not know who did, and I *do* not think it is fair. . . ' If you really can't make the line sound natural, because this dialect is unfamiliar to you, then change 'do not' to 'don't' and 'did not' to 'didn't'.

The same goes for phrases like 'it is not fair'. Stress the

'is' when you read it, but again, if you really can't make it
work, change 'is not' to 'isn't'. If you can manage it, you
will find the phrase almost becomes 'I- *tis*not fair', and in
the North of England this will easily become 'I- *tis*na fair'.

The game

The game that Jan, Mike and Allen play on Reda and Dave
is a little bit like some old-fashioned betrothal ritual.
Clearly they have rehearsed it (and there are clues in the
script to tell us this) at the youth club the night before.
Although the game is lively, and a lot of it tongue-in-cheek,
Jan tries to keep them all in order, and, you will find,
continually tries to give the game a kind of ceremonial
importance. It's a big contrast to her own 'betrothal' —
Mike's rather short invitation to go out with him. Yet, as
you will know from your own experience, it's important
for freely mixing groups of young people to know who's
'going out' with whom and not to trespass on the relationship. We need to know these things if we're not to upset
others — and ourselves — even if formal engagement parties
may be a thing of the past.

Staging

The beginning and end of the play need an open space. The
central section all takes place in a classroom.
     One way of arranging the settings more formally, if you
intend to perform to an audience, might be:

	Classroom	
Audience	Open space	Audience
Audience	Teacher's desk	Audience
Audience		Audience
	Audience	

In order to bring important parts of the action forward,
Jan, Mike and Allen might bring chairs out in front of the

desks so that the 'proposals' game is played in the open space, near the audience. The drawback of this arrangement is that when Mr Redford is on, he will have to play with his back to the audience — or at least some of it. Examine what he has to say and consider how big a drawback this is. After all, in compensation, the reactions to him will be clearly visible on the young people's faces.

Stage lights are not terribly important for this play, but if they are available and set, you might dim them momentarily between scenes, and keep them dim for Jan's party, or perhaps you could set up disco lighting just for this scene.

Discussion and follow-up

1   Discuss relationships which seesaw up and down. Write diaries or poems in which the mood is up and down on successive days or in successive stanzas.

2   Write or improvise scenes which have made you feel like wringing a best friend's neck.

3   Discuss some of the games you play with your friends. Turn them into short dramatic scenes containing the essence of the game.

4   How much do you know about how young people through the ages have 'made dates'? Try to find out from reference books about the social customs of:
     twelfth-century nobility/peasantry
     Roundheads (Puritans) and Cavaliers (pleasure-
          seeking aristocrats)
     prosperous and working-class Victorians
     1920s flappers and 1930s unemployed people
     your parents and . . . you
You could then dramatise 'betrothal' scenes between the characters of one of these periods, as a historical equivalent to this play.

5   Tape-record a group of your friends (and you) talking. Most people hate being recorded secretly, so ask permission and leave the recorder running until they've forgotten it. Try to record casual conversations about

everyday topics — the sort you might have before lessons or over a meal.

Transcribe some sections from the tape (don't attempt too much), trying to write down accurately every word, hesitation, false start, laugh, etc. Let some others act your transcript and tape the result. What have you learnt about the relationship between written and spoken language? And about the relationship between natural and acted speech?

I Tell a Lie

Alan never knows when he's lying. His argument is that he
has been surrounded by lies, liars and hypocrites from his
birth. He has heard so many lies called the truth that he
can't be expected to know the difference. He 'proves' his
point (can liars prove anything?) by asking for scenes from
his past to be re-enacted.

If you think Alan gets off lightly this time, you will
hardly be surprised to learn that he's in the dock for the
sequel to this play *Nothing but the Truth* in the com-
panion volume *Masks and Faces*.

The characters and setting

A strong actor will be needed to play Alan, and you may
prefer to take turns in playing him in different scenes.
(After all, we're all a bit like him, aren't we?) If you do, it
may help to give him a piece of costume — a scarf or a hat
say, or even a half-mask, that each actor playing him can
put on in turn.

Some teachers may be tempted to play Alan, as it's such
a crucial part, but young people do resent this kind of
intrusion. Sharing the part round will probably be better.

In any case, Alan must be played with a light touch, and
the jokes shouldn't be overdone, laboured, or worked to
death. Try to make sure that his speeches flow — despite
the lightning changes of direction from addressing the
audience to talking to the actors, from suddenly 'having an
idea' to cracking a joke. He's got to be chatty, but in
control. And highly mobile throughout.

The other actors who role-play Alan's life should be
ready to leap up at a fraction of a second's notice. For
performance they could be seated in a semicircle, facing the
audience semicircle. They frequently have to improvise
short crowd reactions, for example cooing over the babies
or reacting to Alan's aftershave 'pong'.

In some classrooms, teachers may prefer to keep the class seated at desks. The play will still work well, especially if 'Alan' can be seated at the front — or move —facing the rest of the class.

The lines written are a guide and should be shared by the 'actors' at random, and others added according to improvisation. You will be aware by now that most *Drama Workshop* plays have moments of 'controlled' improvisation.

'The actors break the scene and sit down' — hold the final stage picture for a fraction of a second (a beat), and then you should all move off briskly at the same time. Try not to crowd each other.

If the actors cast to play the commercial are at all embarrassed, it will not work. It must look professional. If this is impossible, perhaps you could replace it with an advert you have written yourself making the same point. (What is the point?)

Staging

It's a very 'proppy' play. Make a list with props in one column and where each one is to be set in another column.

All the props need to be carefully placed to be at hand the moment they are needed.

For lighting, you probably need to decide whether to play it all in the same light, or to go for very many changes done very slickly. There isn't really an in-between.

'Auntie Doris rings the doorbell' — this might be a tape-recording or someone might rig up an old doorbell with a battery and pushbutton, in which case we could see her press it as she stands in one of the entrances.

Discussion and follow-up

1   What different sorts of lies are there? List as many as you can think of. Then try to sort them in order of gravity, or badness.

    Dramatise some of the lies and invent scenes which show the consequences of the lies.

2   Do you think Alan can be any kind of friend to any-one?

3   Do you think Alan has got a point in the play, or is he just making excuses?

4   What is the difference — if any — between telling lies and being a liar?

5   There's an old paradox summed up in the question, 'When a liar says he's a liar, can you believe him?' What do you think? And can you say what a paradox is?

6   Invent a character who thinks all lies are wicked. Basing it on one of the scenes in the play, write a dialogue between this person and Alan as they discuss or argue whether the lie was justified or not.

      If different people or groups work on different pieces of dialogue, you could rewrite and then re-enact the whole play in this way.

7   Imagine a relationship — family, business or friendship — in which one of the partners has for a long time been deceiving the others. Finally he (or she) slips up and is discovered. Write a chapter describing the event, which could be part of a longer novel. (You may need to sketch out briefly the events of the earlier chapters.) Try to base the characters on real people you know, rather than on characters from television.

Hands Off!

At first sight, this seems like a documentary about the flooding of a Welsh valley and the protest which accompanies it. As you get to know the play, you will find that in fact it's a comedy, and at the end, when the TV crew get what they deserve (and more!) it becomes black comedy. It's also about the life of a close community, and the importance of respecting our neighbours' views and beliefs.

Acting and the characters

You will probably find the play is more effective if the villagers are played with Welsh or regional accents, or at least played in voices that are noticeably gentler, more good-humoured and more musical than the brash TV style of Mike, the commentator. The way he speaks is not unlike the language of Alan Whicker, a television journalist you may remember.

One of the things to be enjoyed about the villagers is their eccentricity. Hugh Pugh's decision to build an ark seems entirely appropriate, looked at from the point of view of a man who sees the whole world through the Bible's Old Testament. Equally the Evans's logic in drawing out all their savings and investing in a larder full of groceries has its own stubborn logic. We laugh at these eccentricities, but we may also feel a certain sadness, because there is something important in the way these people plan to survive in the face of an immense decision made hundreds of miles away. For this reason, it's important not to play these characters for laughs. They themselves are totally serious about what they plan to do. Let the audience — if you perform the play — find the humour for themselves; don't give it to them on a plate. In other words, don't belittle the characters. They don't deserve it.

The speakers at the public enquiry are obviously serious.

The important thing if you are acting them is to be sure you understand the points they are making. You will need to convey the meaning with sincerity and you will be attempting to win the audience over to your point of view.

There are several opportunities for crowd scenes. 'Coming out of the chapel' is straightforward, but work out details of who you are in the crowd. However small the part you play, you should be able to give considerable details in answer to a question like, 'Who are you?' (Age, occupation, temperament, relationships with others, daily habits, etc.)

'Angry protesting villagers' — you need to plan the attitudes of each individual protester before you start. Possible attitudes might be:

I don't want to lose my home under water

I have nowhere else to go

I'd like to be rehoused, but they'll have to pay

To set the characters, during rehearsals, you could improvise scenes between them, as though before the meeting. Do some of them group their protests together, invent chants, etc?

All crowd scenes should be tackled in this kind of way if they are not to seem sketchy.

Even if all the village people need to be played fairly close to life, you can allow yourself to have more fun with the TV crew. They are self-conscious, limelight-seeking people anyway. The one moment when we see their true selves is when realisation dawns on them at the end. Then it will be a challenge to anyone playing these parts not to overact and clearly to show the real person under the public figure.

Staging

It will help if you can set up a multiple setting for performance, just as for class work. You could try the kind of setting used in medieval morality plays, where the central area belongs to whichever setting starts off a particular scene:

                              Chapel

        Audience   Audience

    Shop/post-office   Village-hall platform

                          Open central
        Audience   area (or 'place')   Audience

    Price's cottage   Pugh's cottage

        Audience   Audience

                      Evans' cottage

Actors start the scene in their particular 'house'
('mansion', medieval people used to call it) and move out
into the central area if they need to. For example, when
people stream out of the chapel at the beginning of the
play, the central area (which medieval people called the
'place') becomes the street in front of the chapel.

In some cases, actors walk from one scene into the
next. For example, after Scene 8 in the post office, Albert
can be waiting with the wheelbarrow; he and his wife can
load up, walk across to their cottage (they should have set
step-ladder and tools before going shopping) and start
Scene 9.

You will find this sort of staging very fluid and easy to
use, and valuable as a transition from classroom drama to a
simple presentational form.

One problem to be solved is the transition from Scene 1
to Scene 2. Perhaps the last part of the interview can be
tape-recorded and the extract faded up as Scene 2 begins.
Of course the Evans' house will need to be furnished with a
'television'.

(If you find yourself getting interested in medieval
theatre, look up some theatre history books. A good introduction is Richard Southern's *The Seven Ages of Theatre*
(Faber), which will tell you about medieval English plays
(pages 98 to 110), and much more besides. You will find
that the other main English method of staging was on
pageant wagons which trundled through the narrow streets
of northern cities such as Chester, York and Wakefield,

stopping at important 'stations' like the market square, main crossroads, the cathedral square, etc., where the actors would perform the play afresh each time.)

Sound effects

There are a lot of sound effects, and they are important. so it would be worth designating an FX crew. They'll have fun!

You can use discs, or make live sounds, or use your own recordings.

For the tolling bell, you could suspend a metal pipe with string or wire, so that it hangs freely. Strike it with a fairly substantial beater.

Thunder can be made with a large sheet of thin metal (you can often get sheet aluminium from DIY shops), or even cardboard or thick (building) paper or brown paper. You can fix it to hang down, and to work it, give the bottom corners sharp tugs to send a 'ripple' over the sheet. Each flap will create a thunder crack and roll.

If you can't get a big enough sheet, try using a microphone and amplifier, but keep the microphone at the edge of the sheet where it can respond to the sound without 'popping' as puffs of air hit it.

For rain you can experiment with quantities of dried peas or rice sprinkled onto a drum. Add sandpaper rubbed together. Double up these sounds or amplify them, and add vocal effects and perhaps a drum roll for the final catastrophe!

Boffins may know how to use sound synthesisers (or home computers with SOUND commands) to add to the above effects.

Follow-up and discussion

1   What are the rights and wrongs of flooding valleys to make reservoirs? Is there a basic unfairness because the people who benefit are not the same as the people who suffer? Is the matter complicated by the fact that Wales is — some would argue — a different country from England, where the water is usually destined?

2   How would you react if your town or community was earmarked for destruction, either as in the play, or to build, say, a new power station? What could you do to express your reactions practically?

3   Invent scenes in other cottages as people react to the news of the proposed flooding.

4   (i) As one of the villagers, write a letter of protest or acceptance to the local paper.
(ii) Try to write a balanced editorial for the local paper.
(iii) As the MP covering the valley (and probably a much wider area), write a letter to a national newspaper, setting out your views about the proposed flooding.

5   As chairman of the enquiry write a report on it to the Minister of State for the Environment, who will have the final say on whether the flooding is to go ahead.

6   Prepare a speech to be made by you as leader of a deputation to the Minister of State. Remember that you are unlikely to get anywhere by bluster, but you may be able to sway him with persuasive argument well put. Role-play the meeting.

7   Like the Evans's, you decide to barricade yourself in your cottage in the face of the police and Electricity Board officials. Write a diary of the siege.

8   As a policeman who has had to evict villagers from their homes, write an official report for your superiors and then set down your personal feelings in a letter to your mother, or tell them to a good friend.

9   Write a poem as if you are fifteen or twenty years in the future contemplating the still waters of the reservoir. You might choose to write an elegy — a poem of lamentation for the community that used to exist — or you might write as a city poet who is only too glad to have escaped the suffocation of the narrow life in villages, and has no regrets at all about the 'drowning' of this particular village.